COLOR TEST PAGE

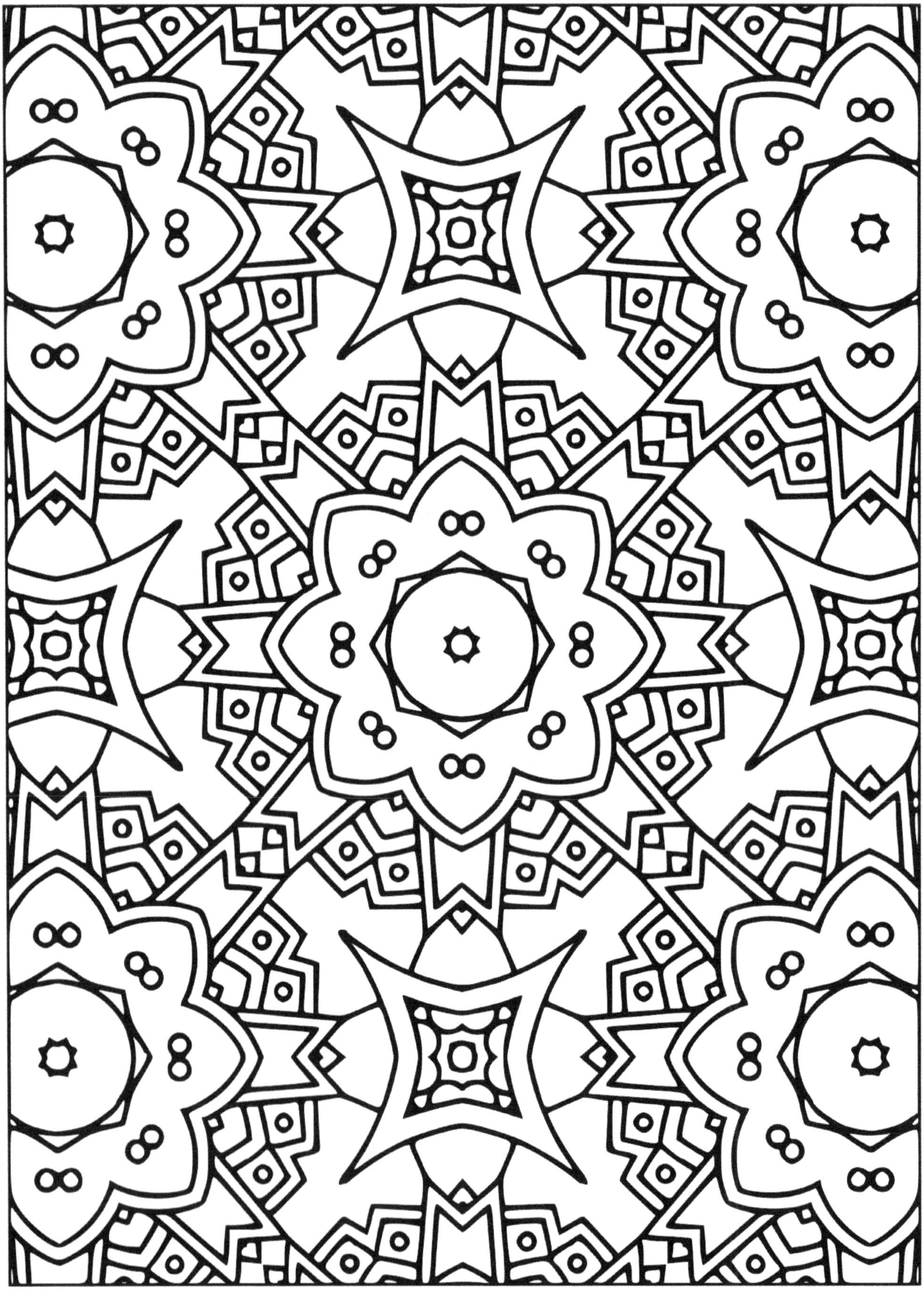

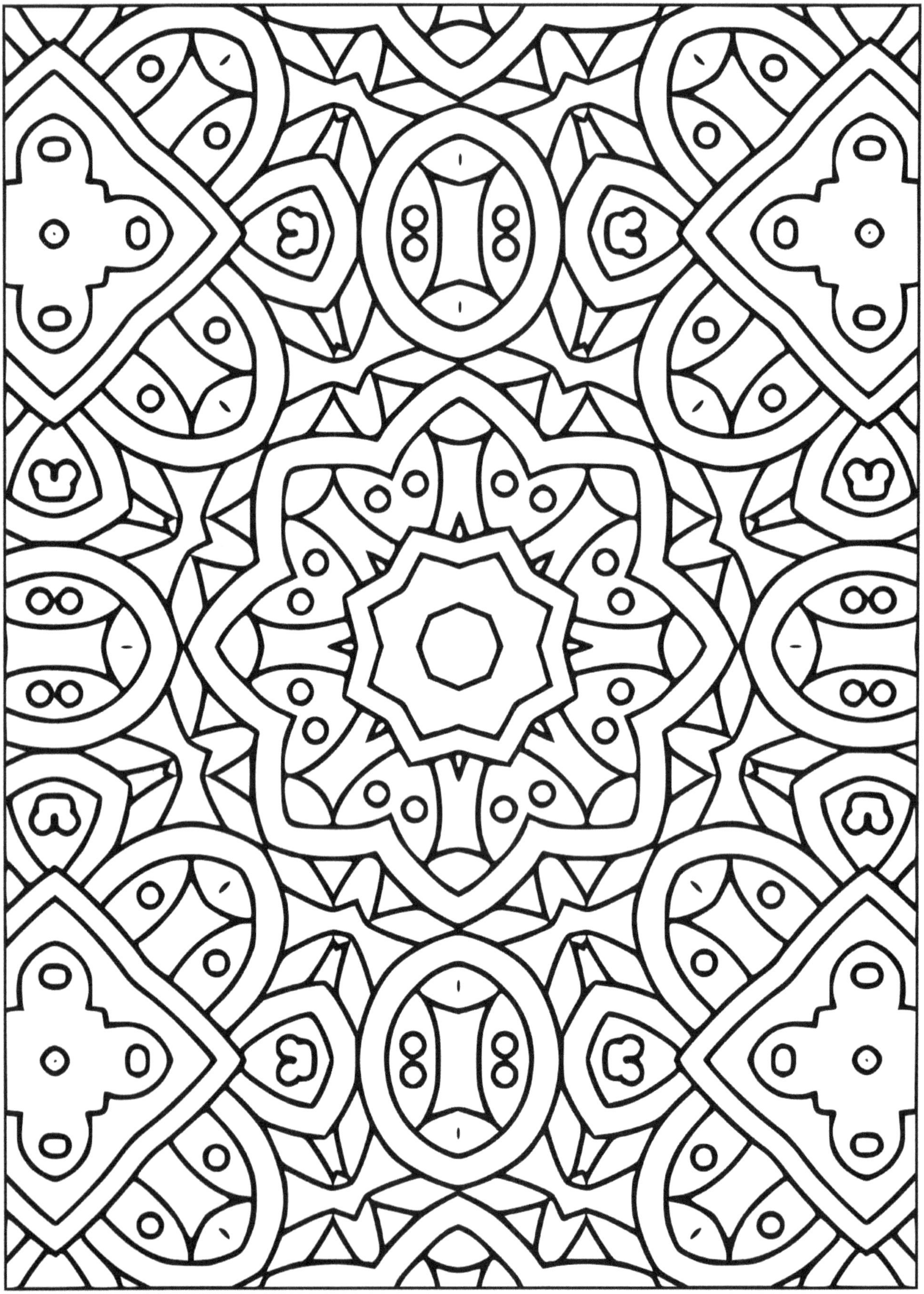

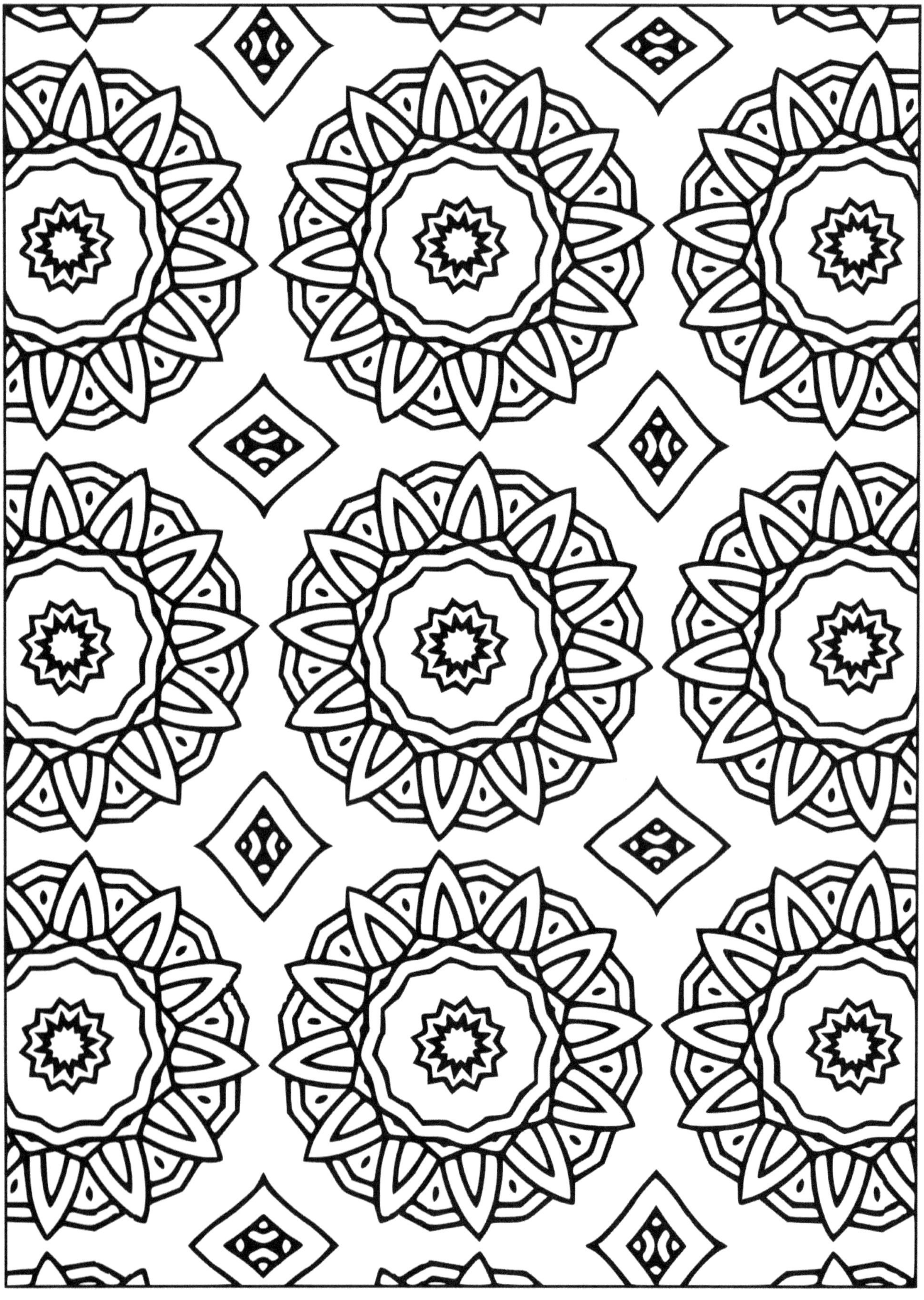

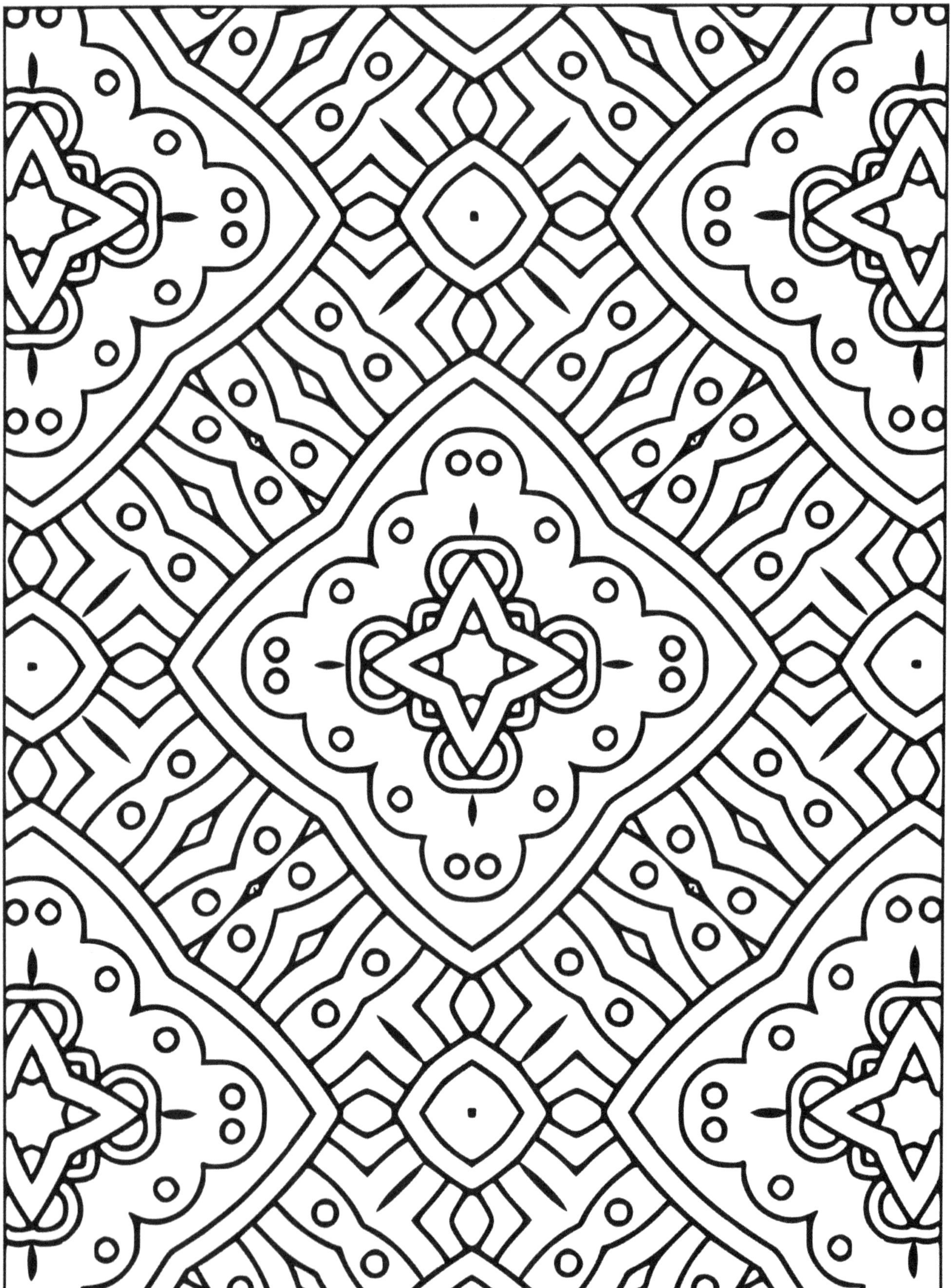

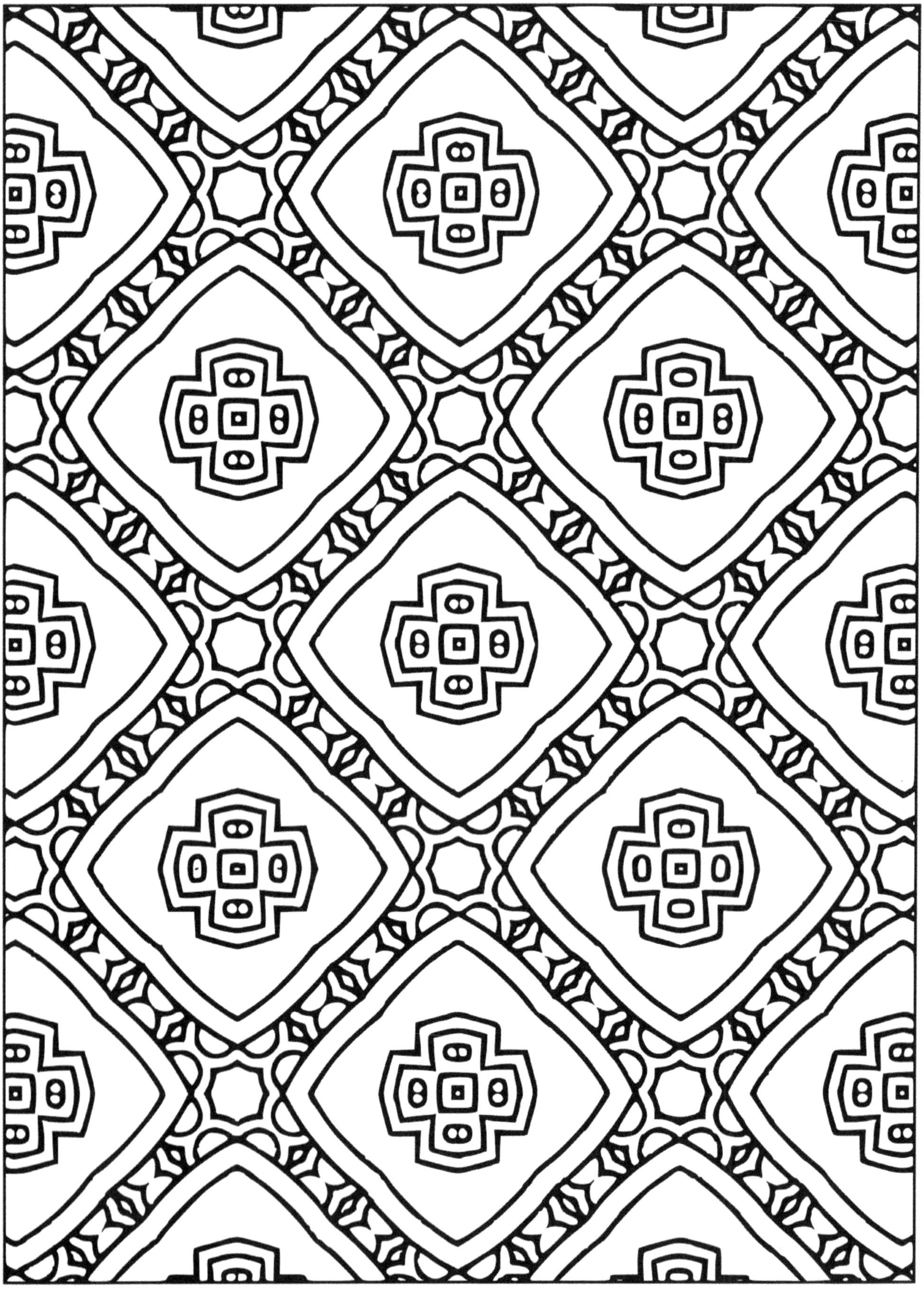

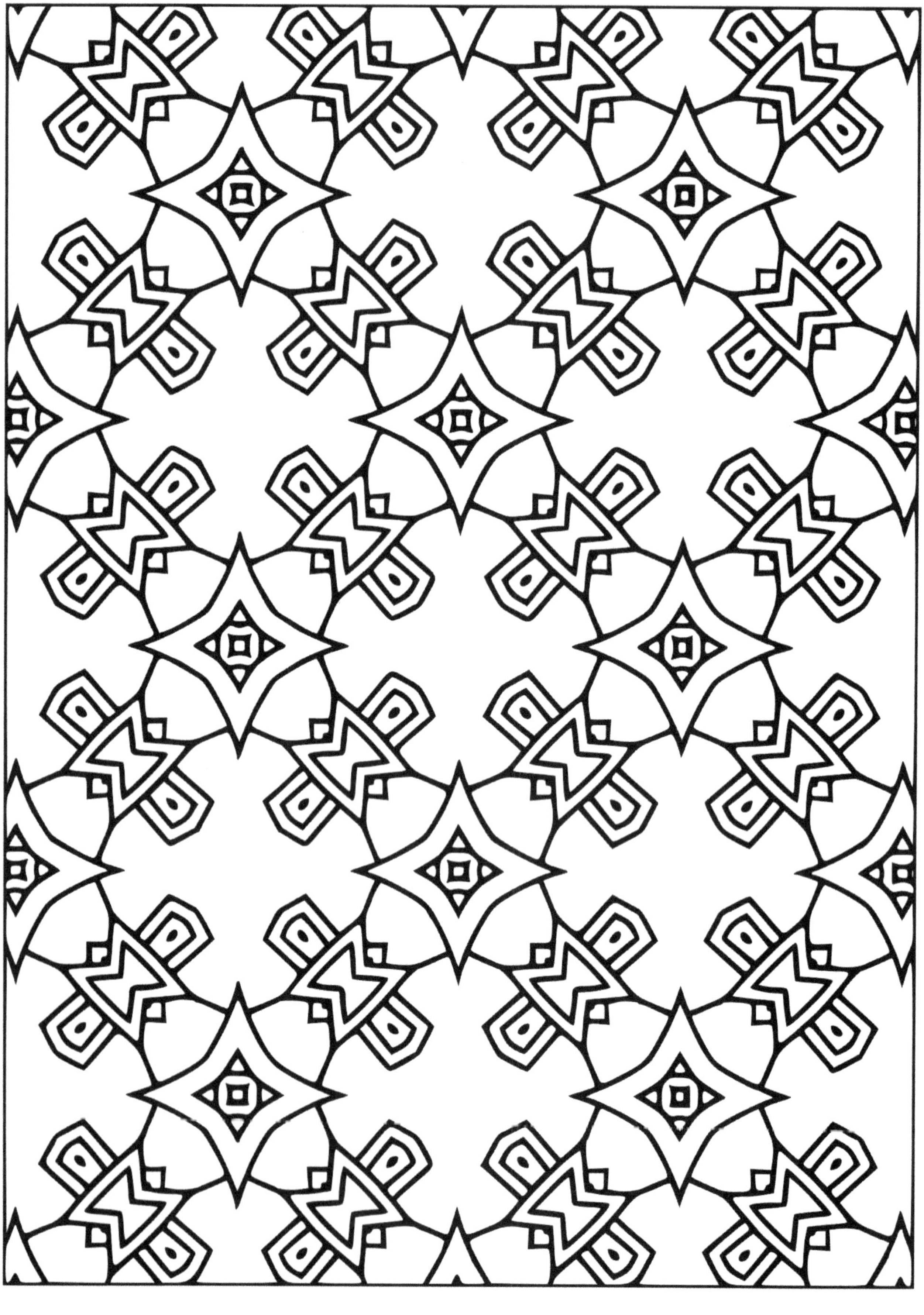

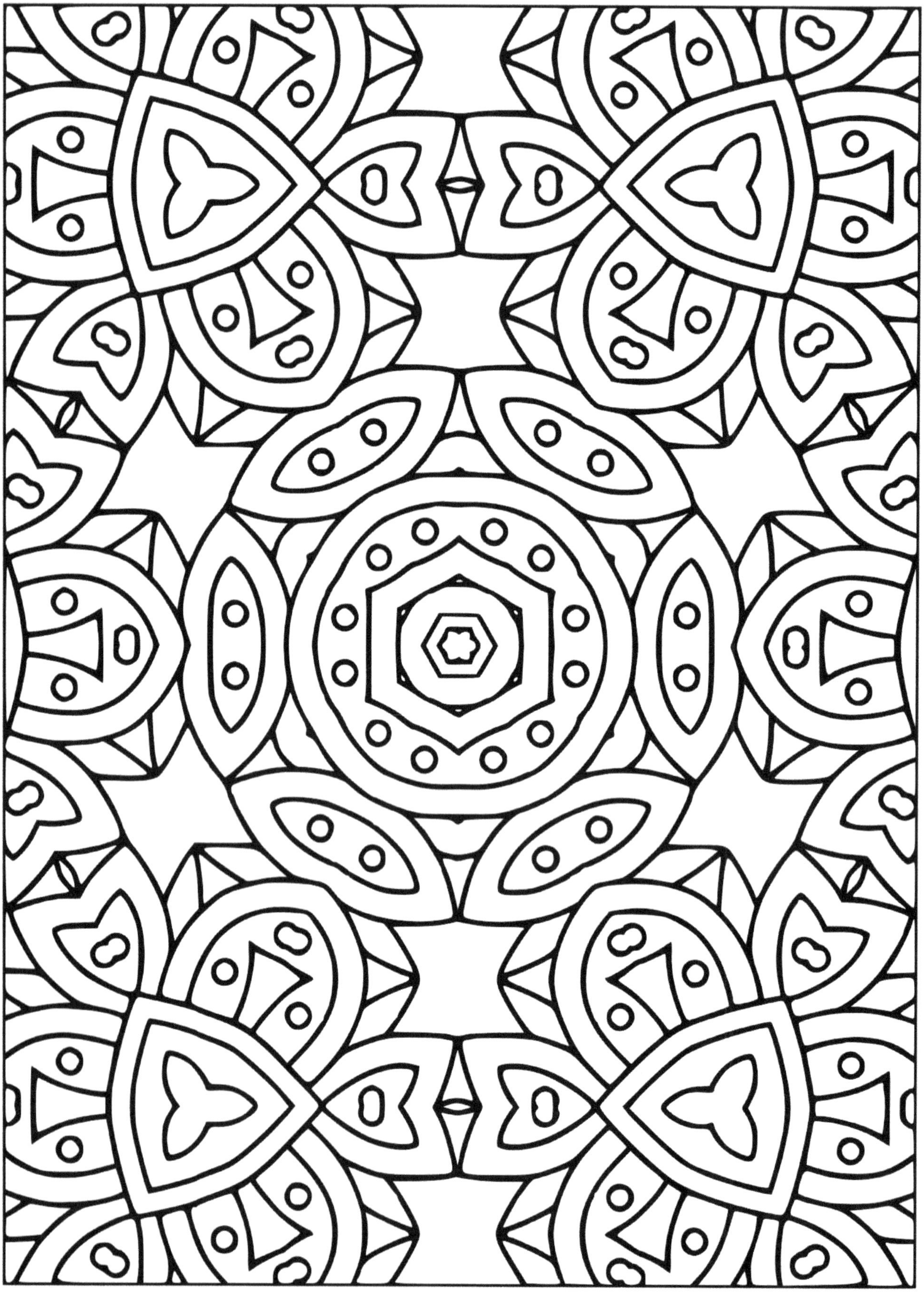

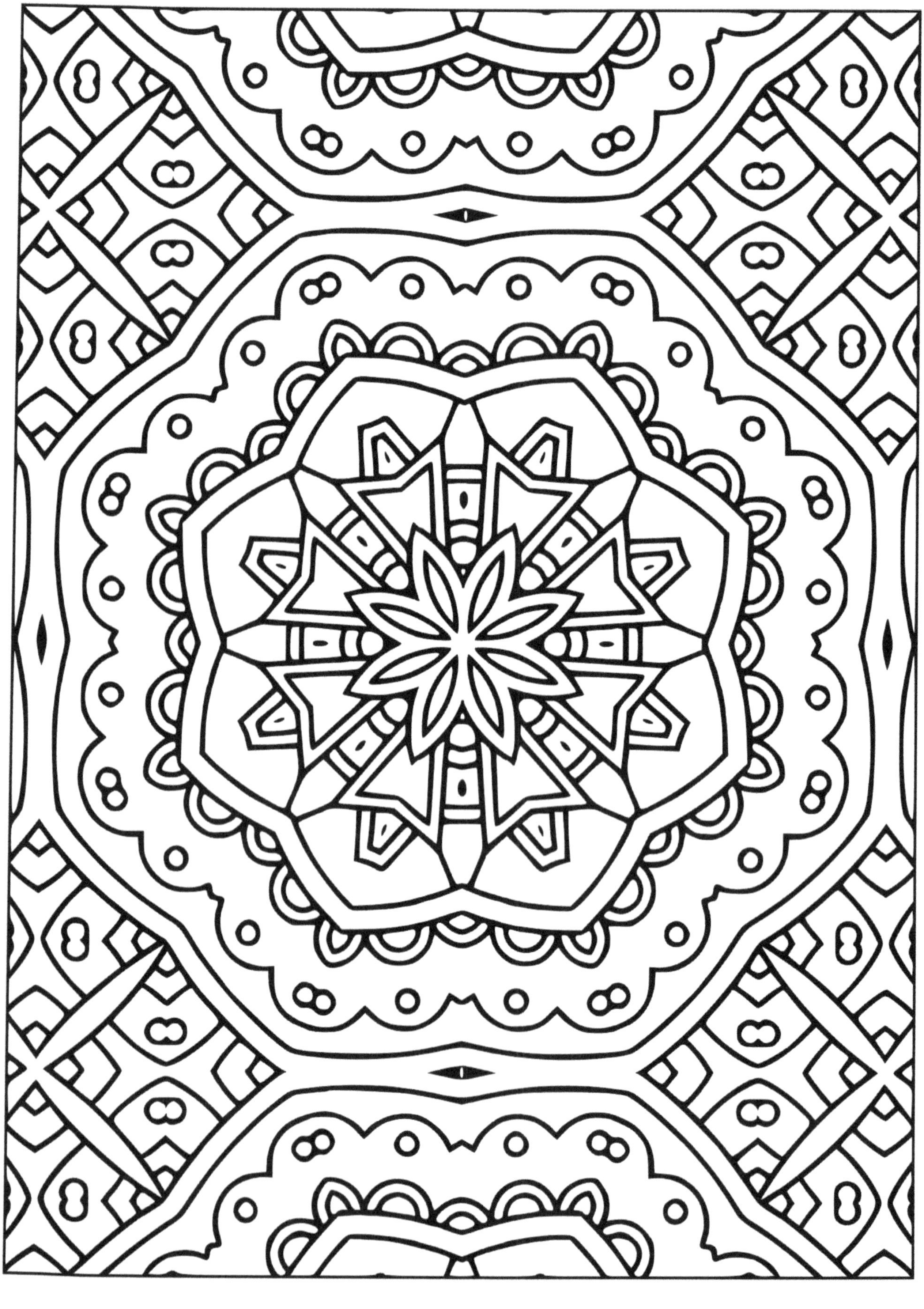

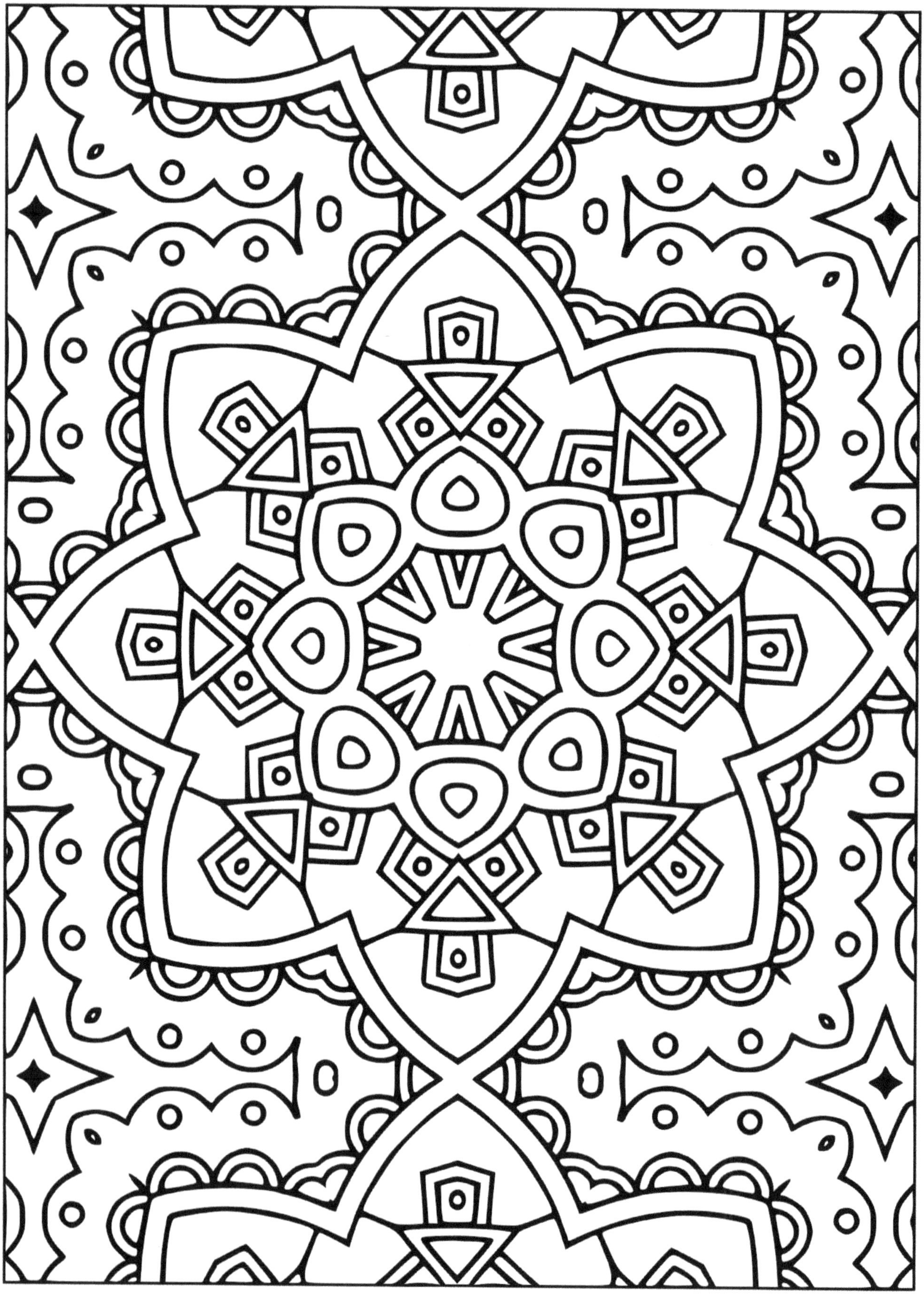

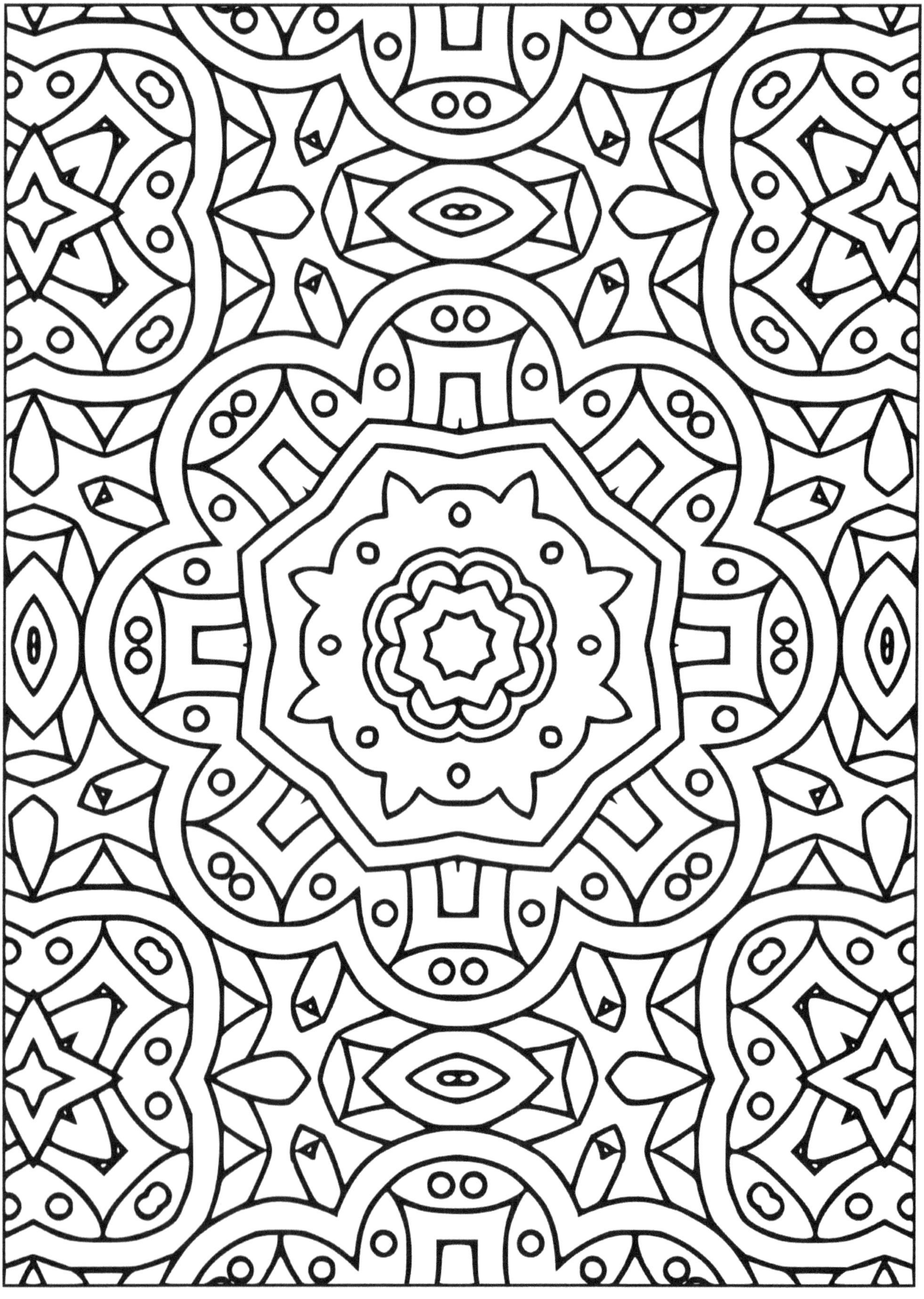

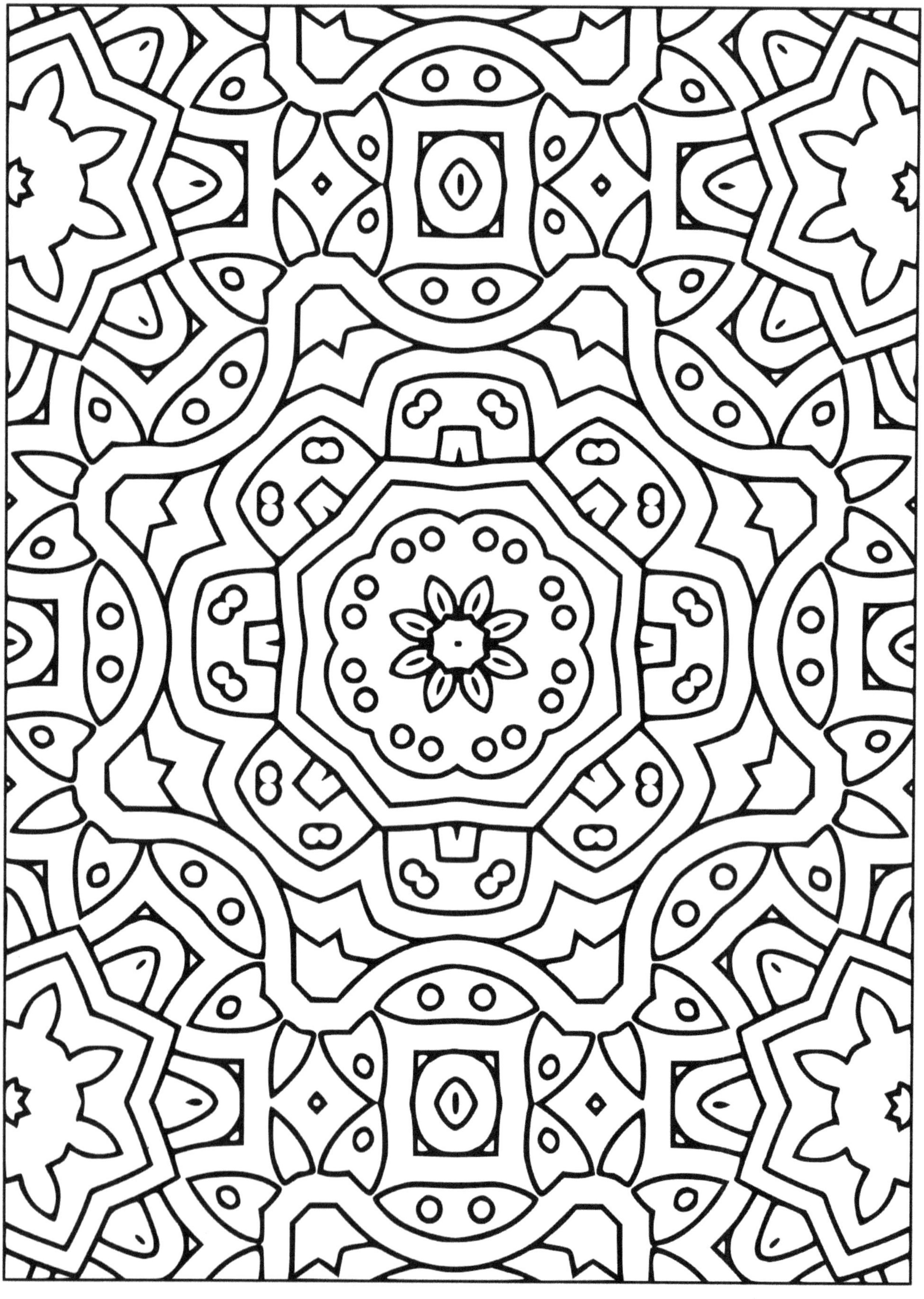

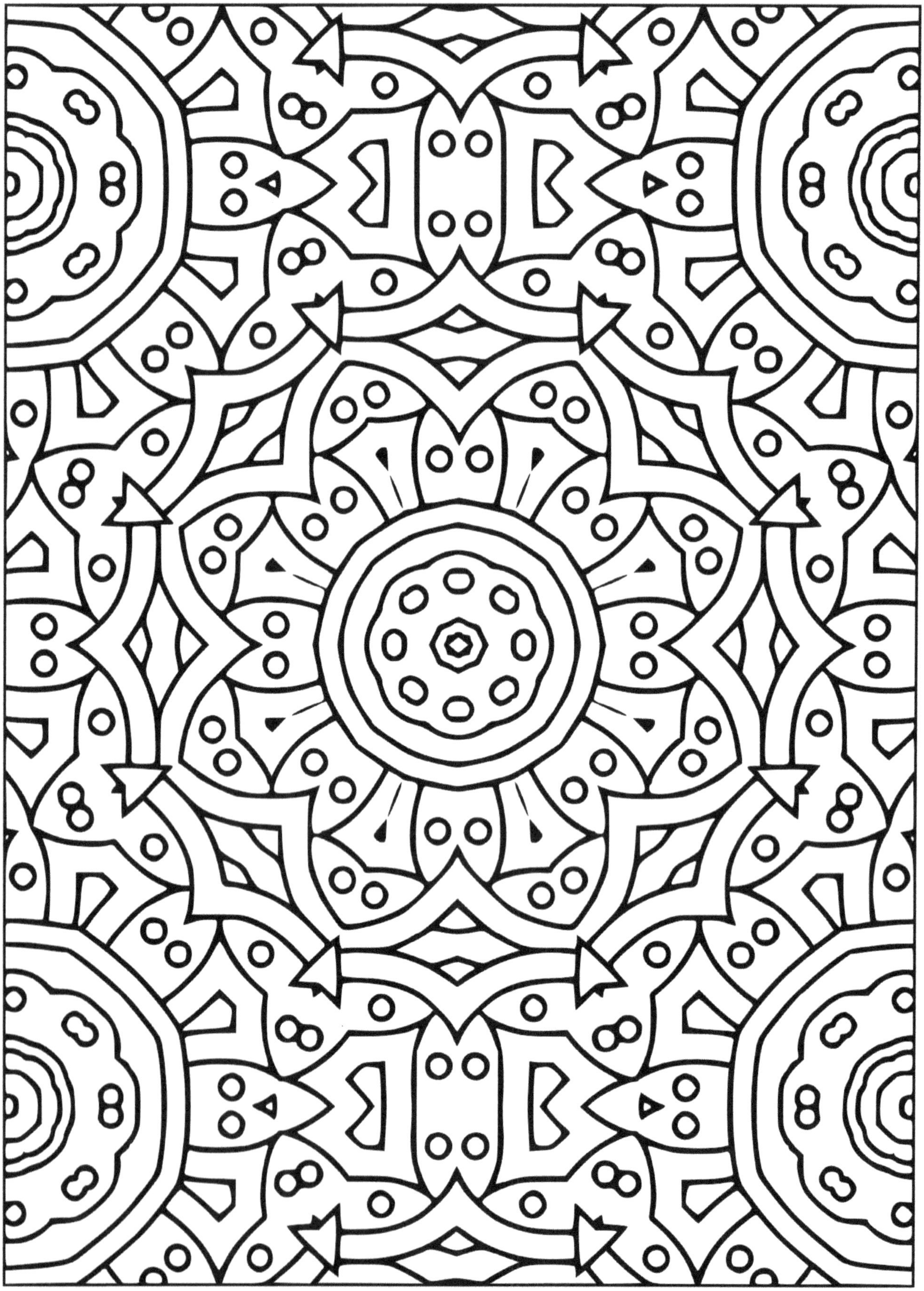

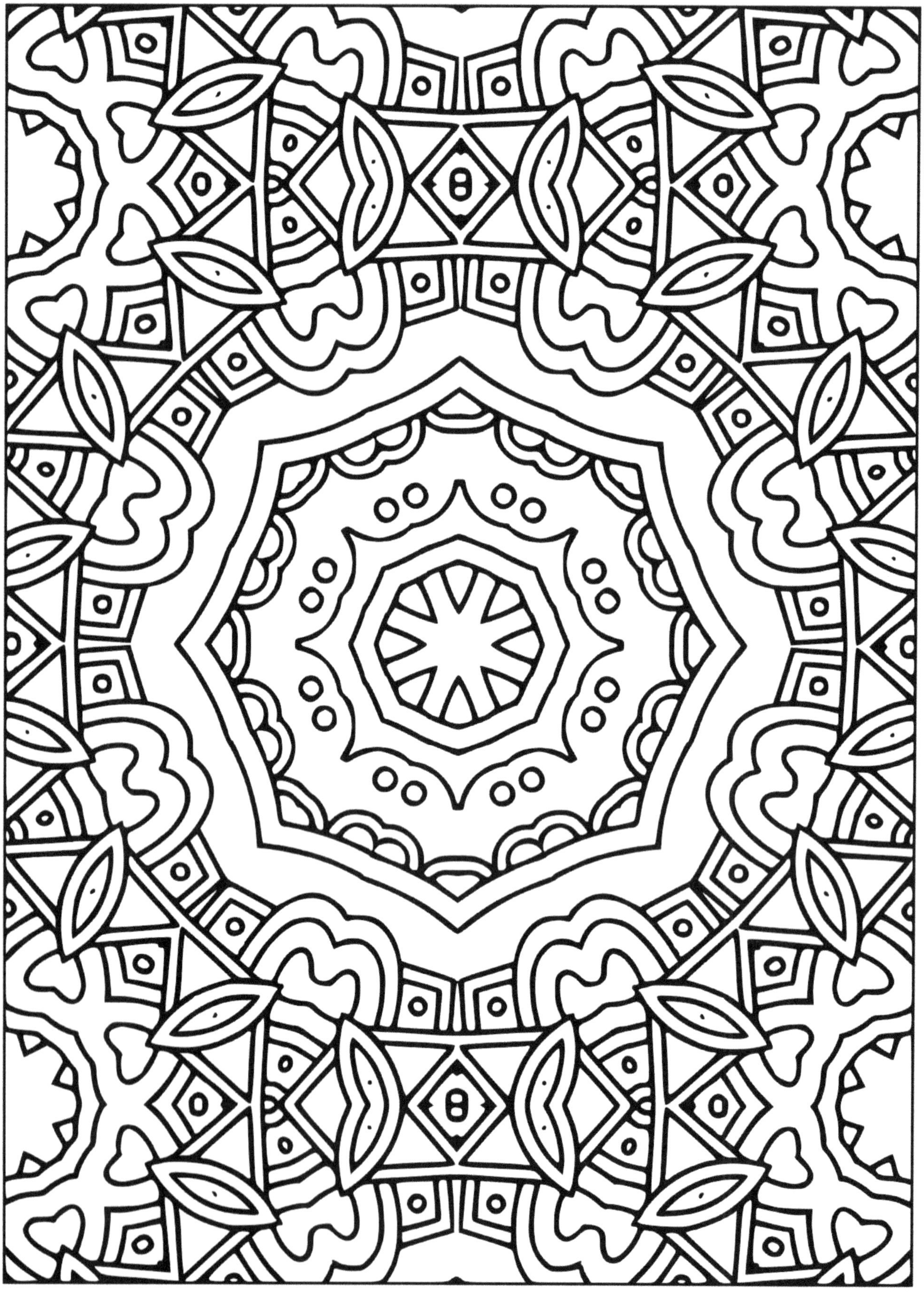

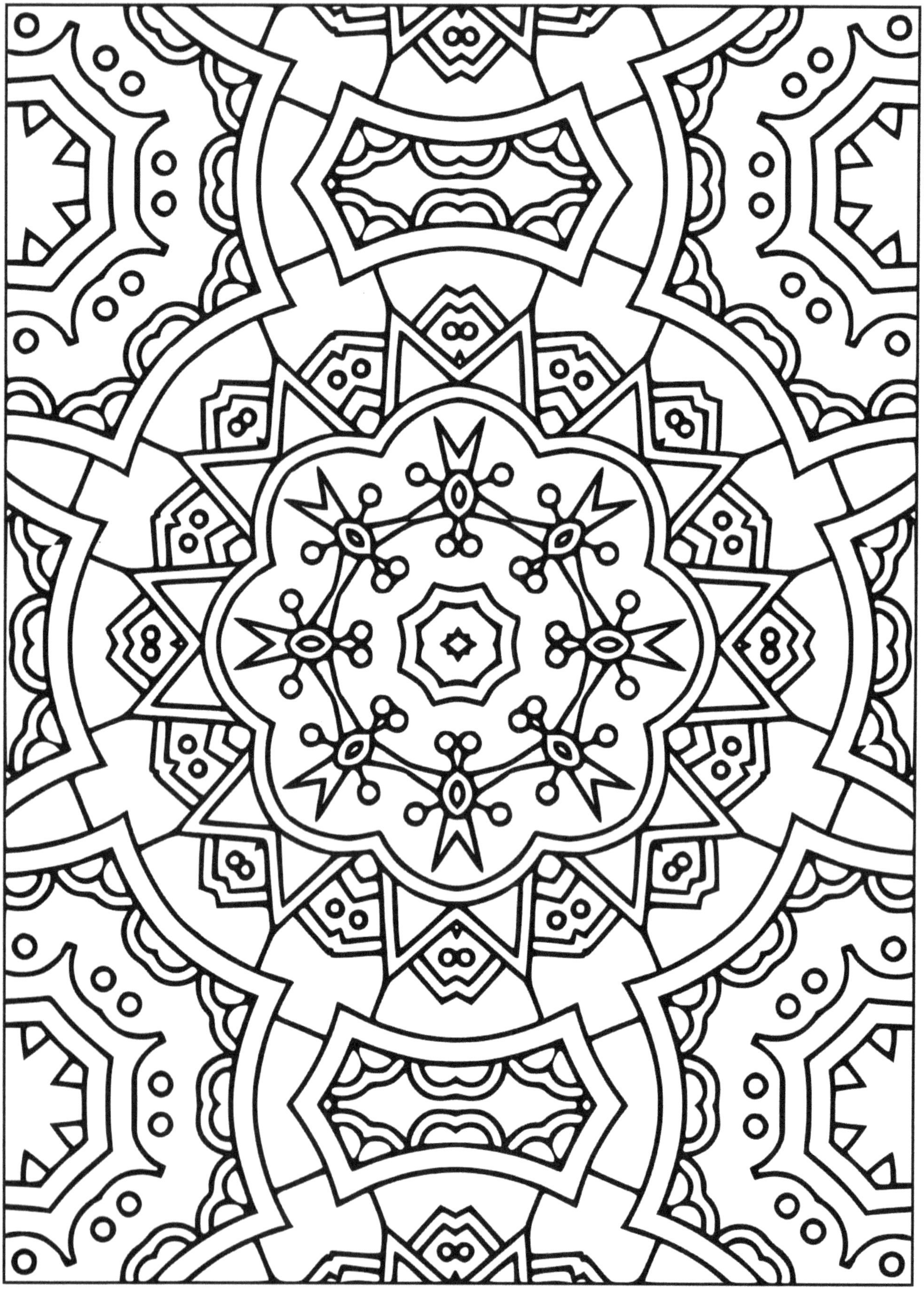

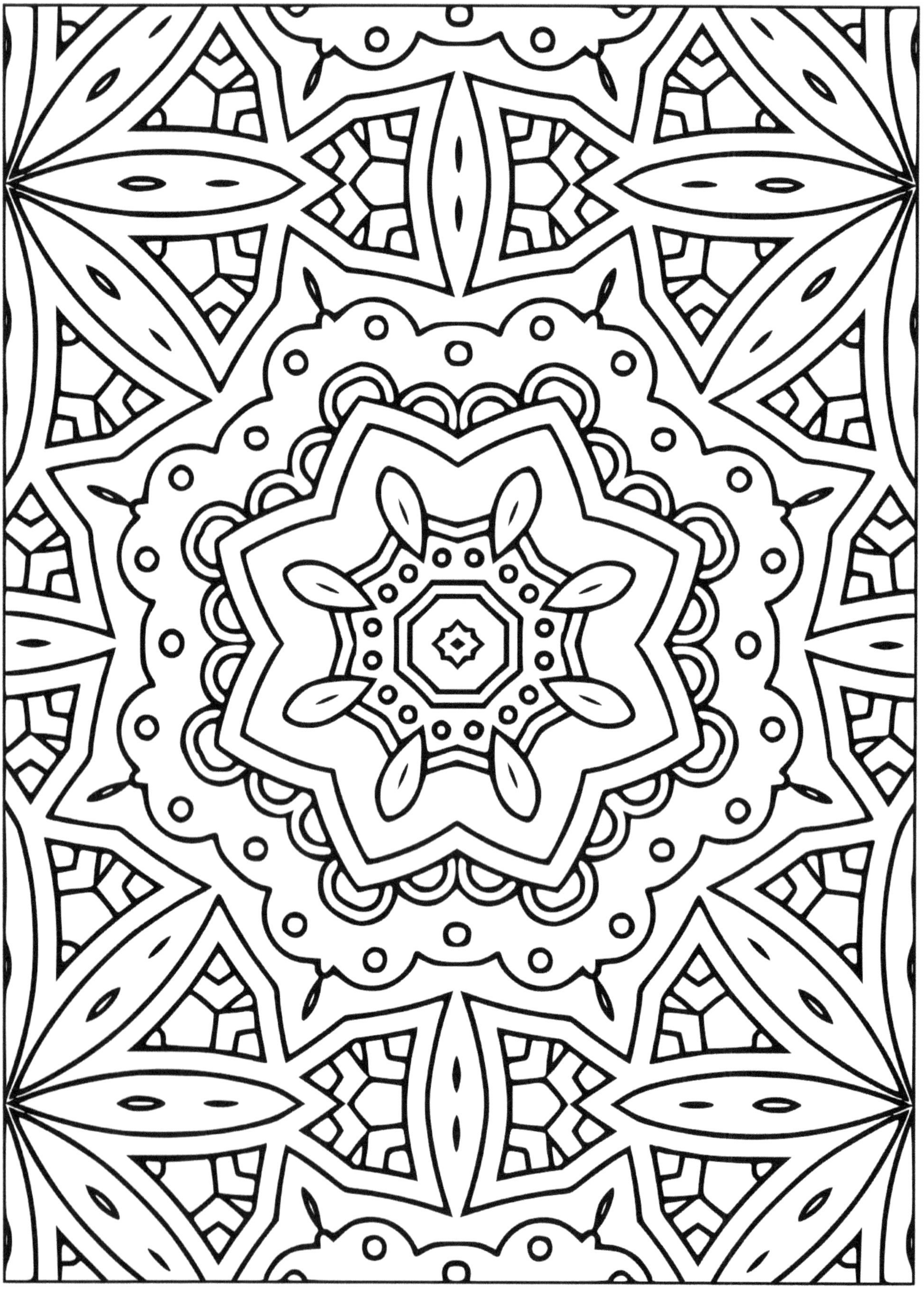

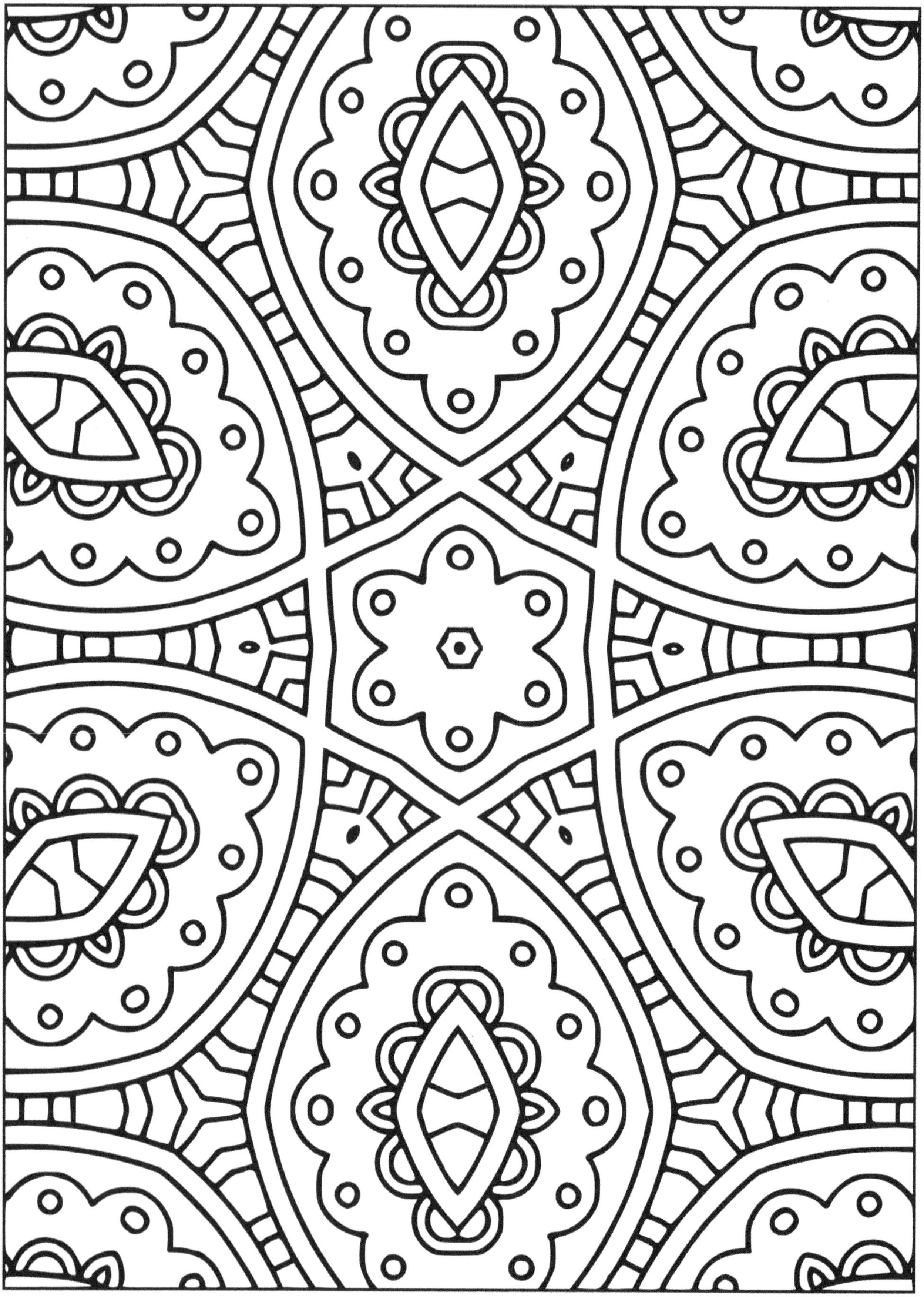

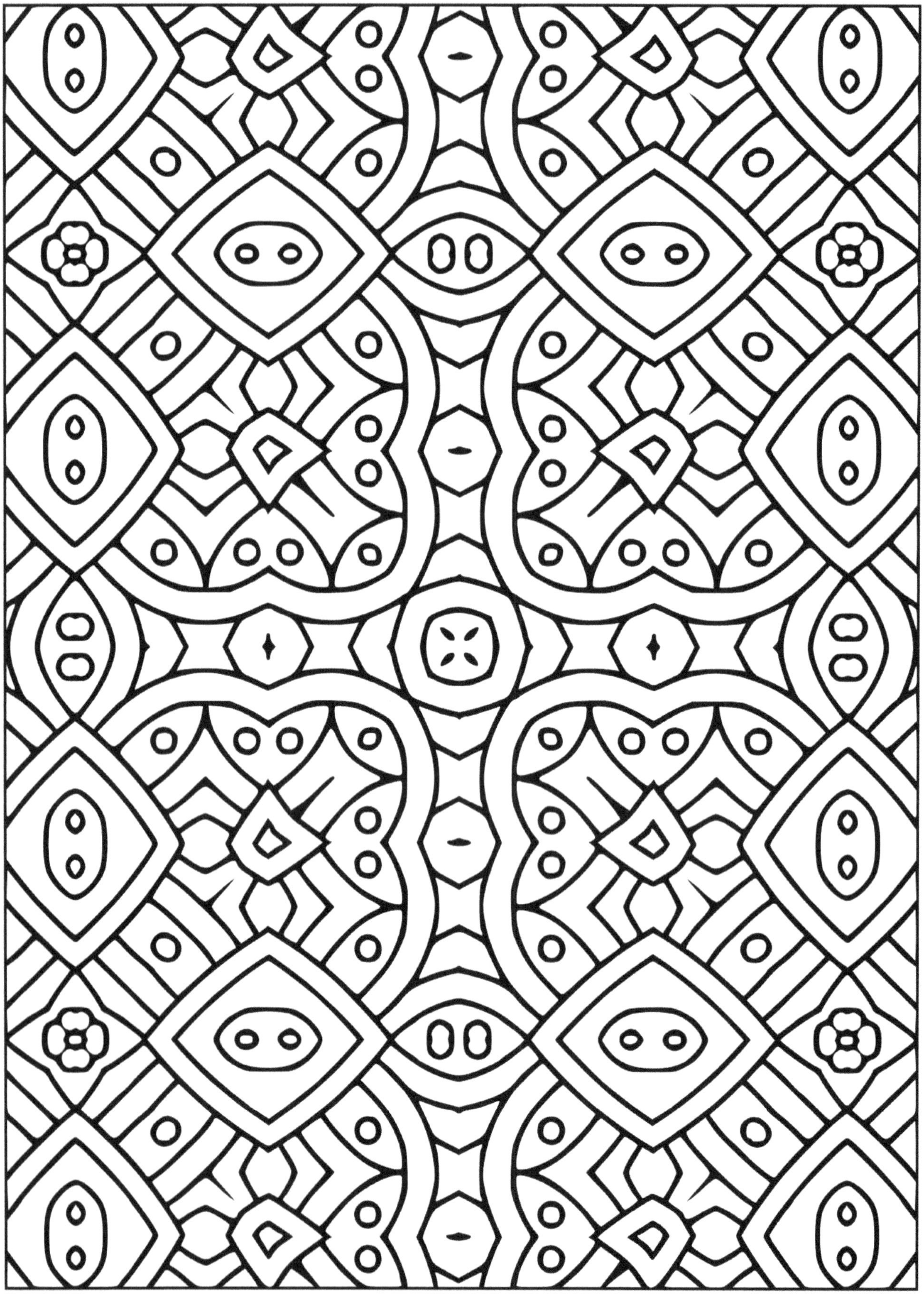

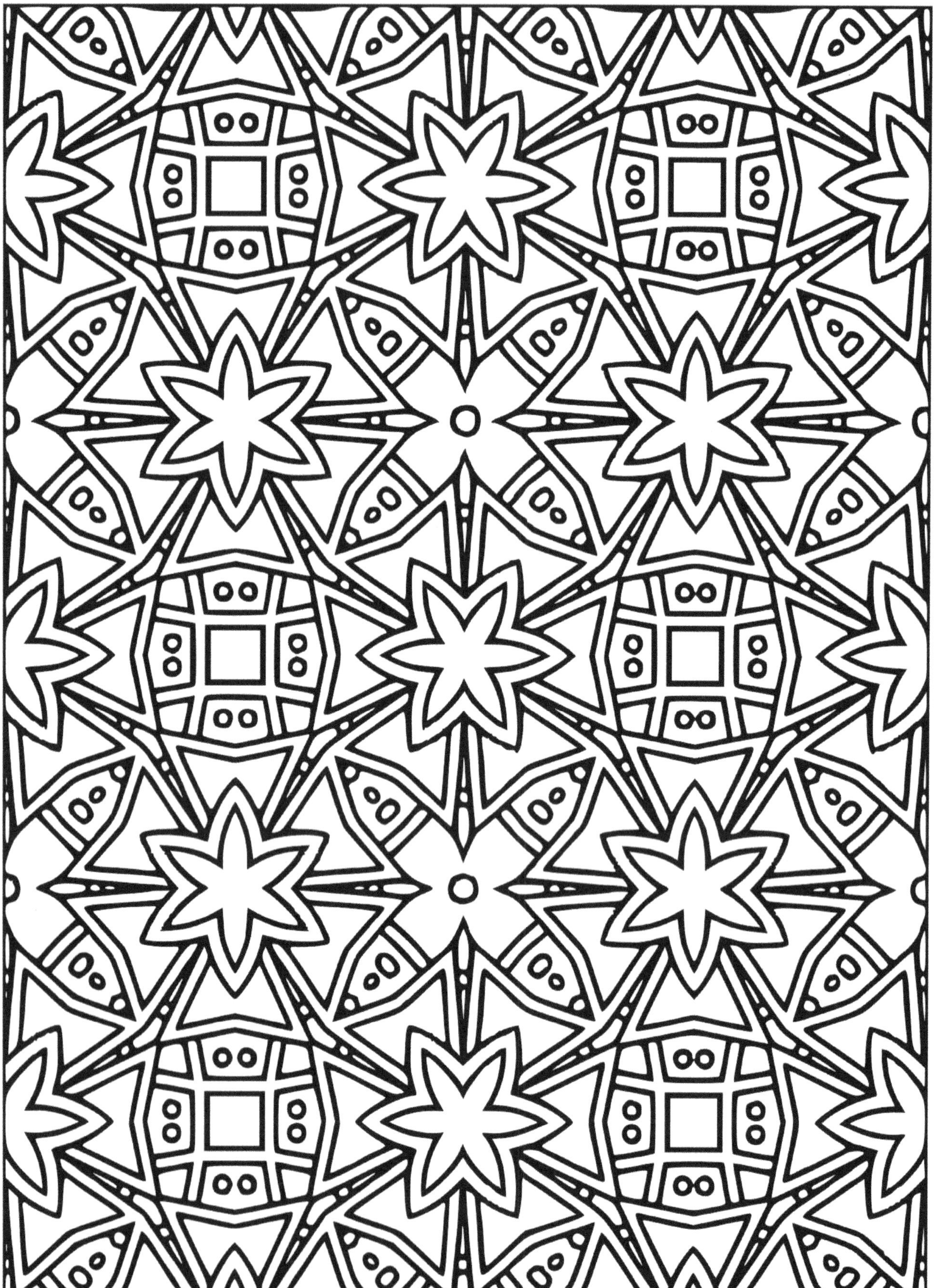

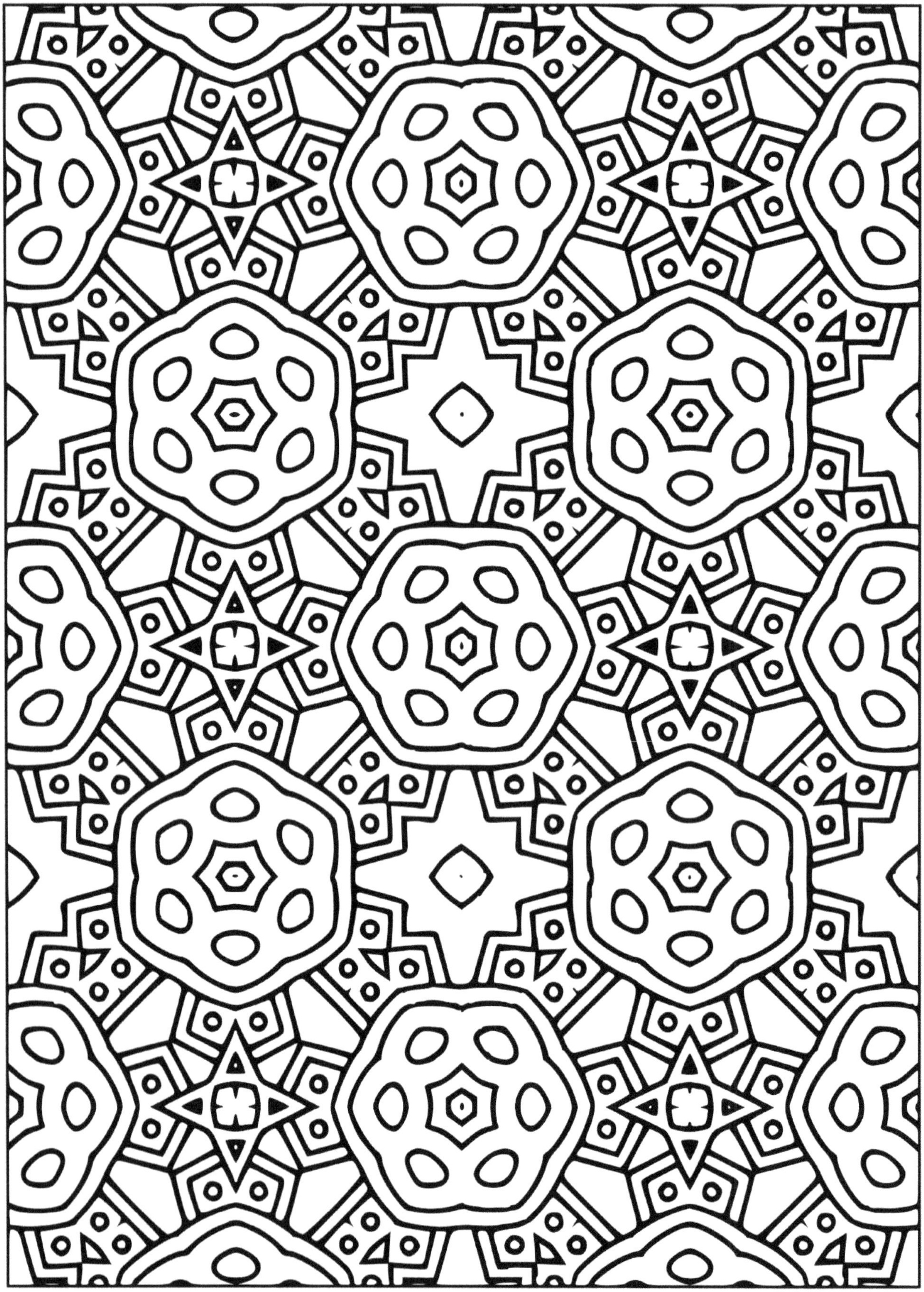

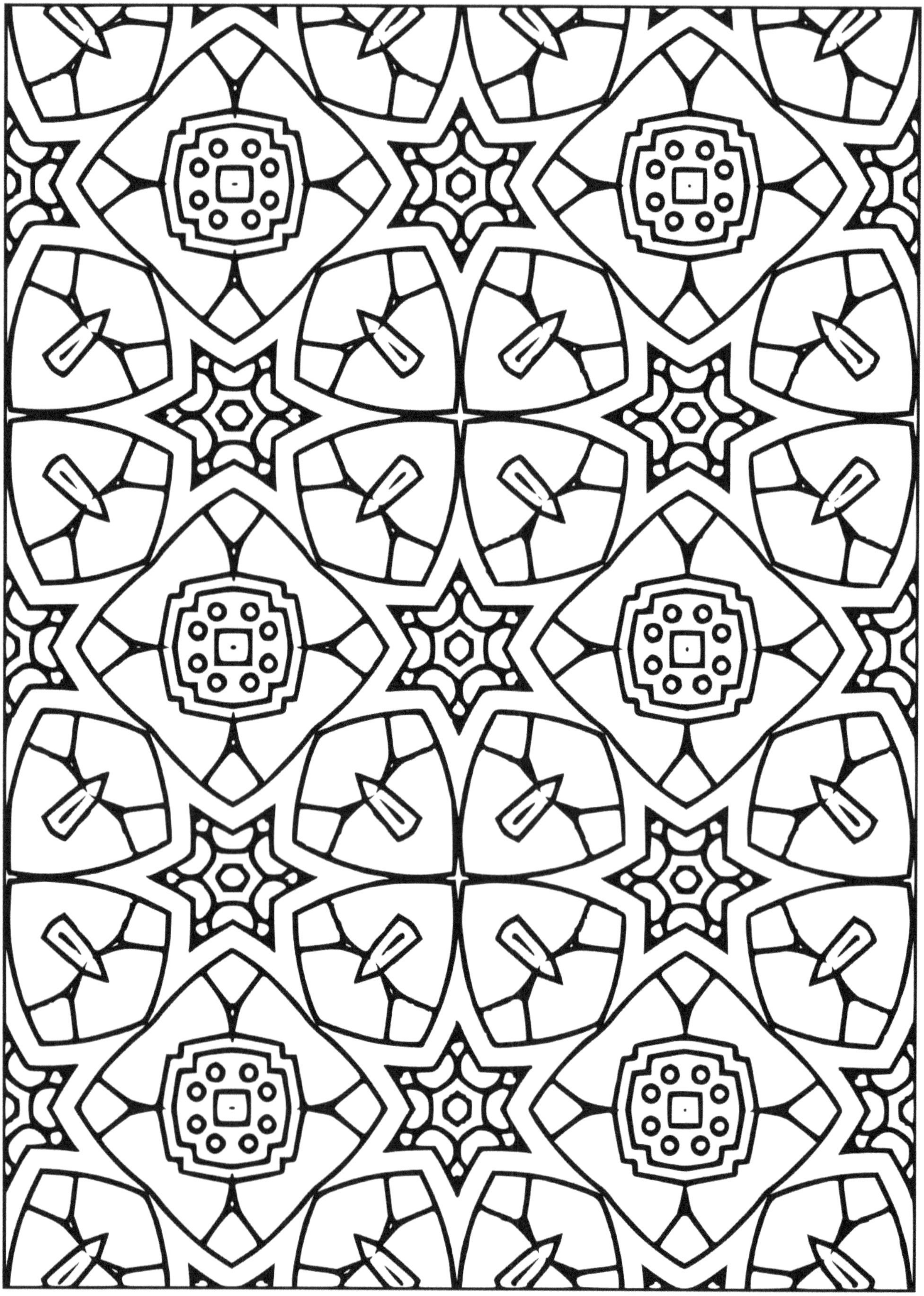

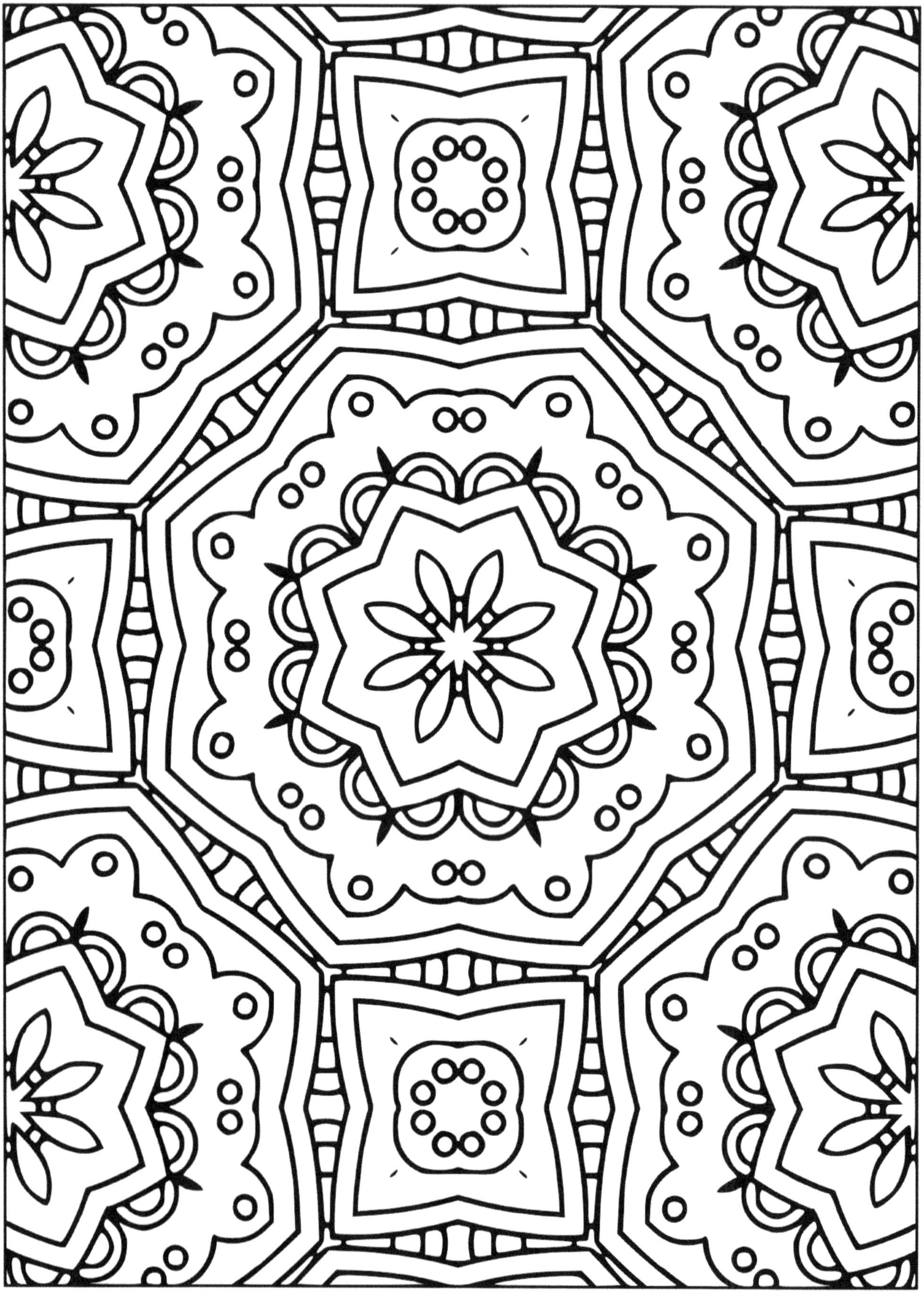

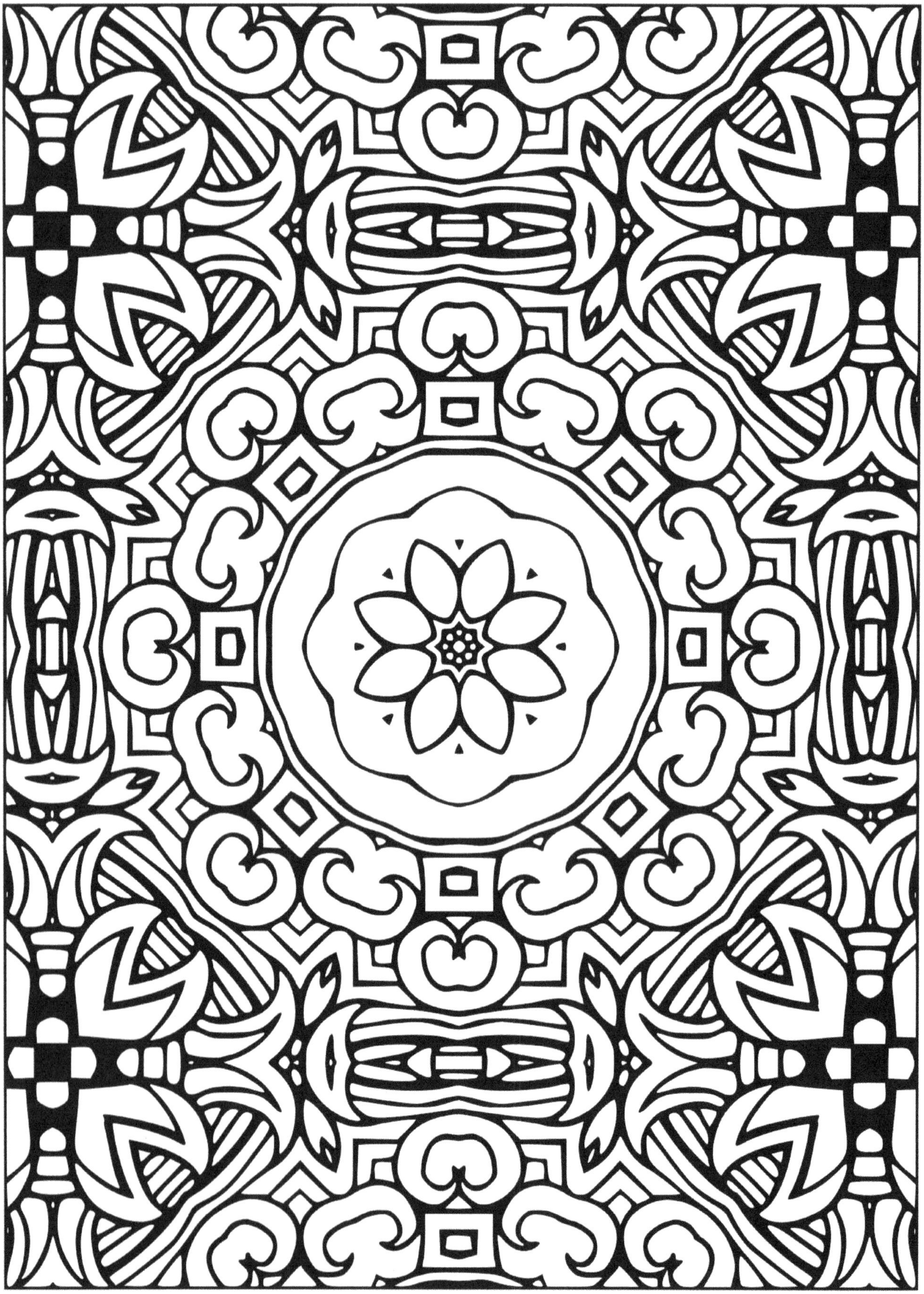

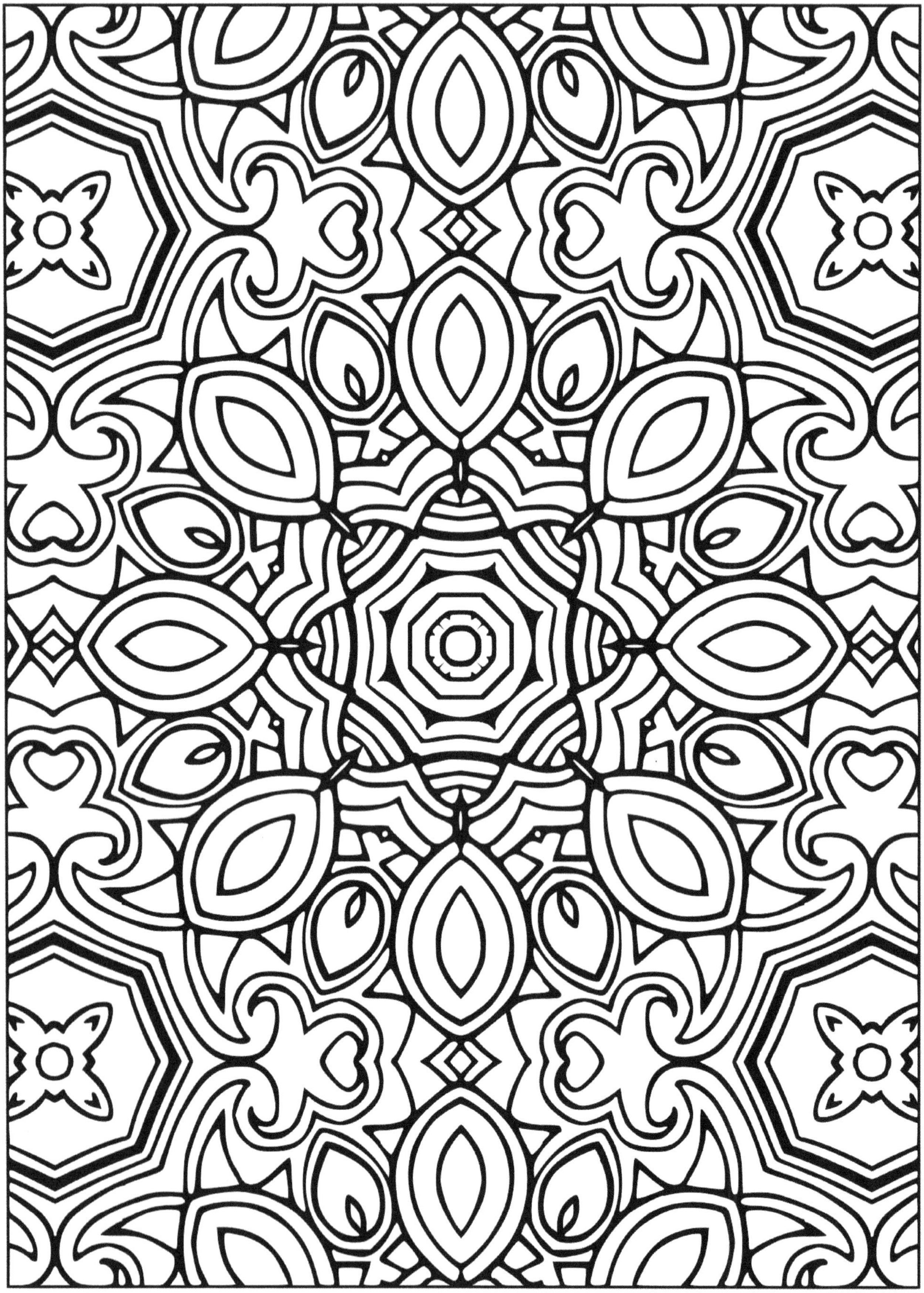

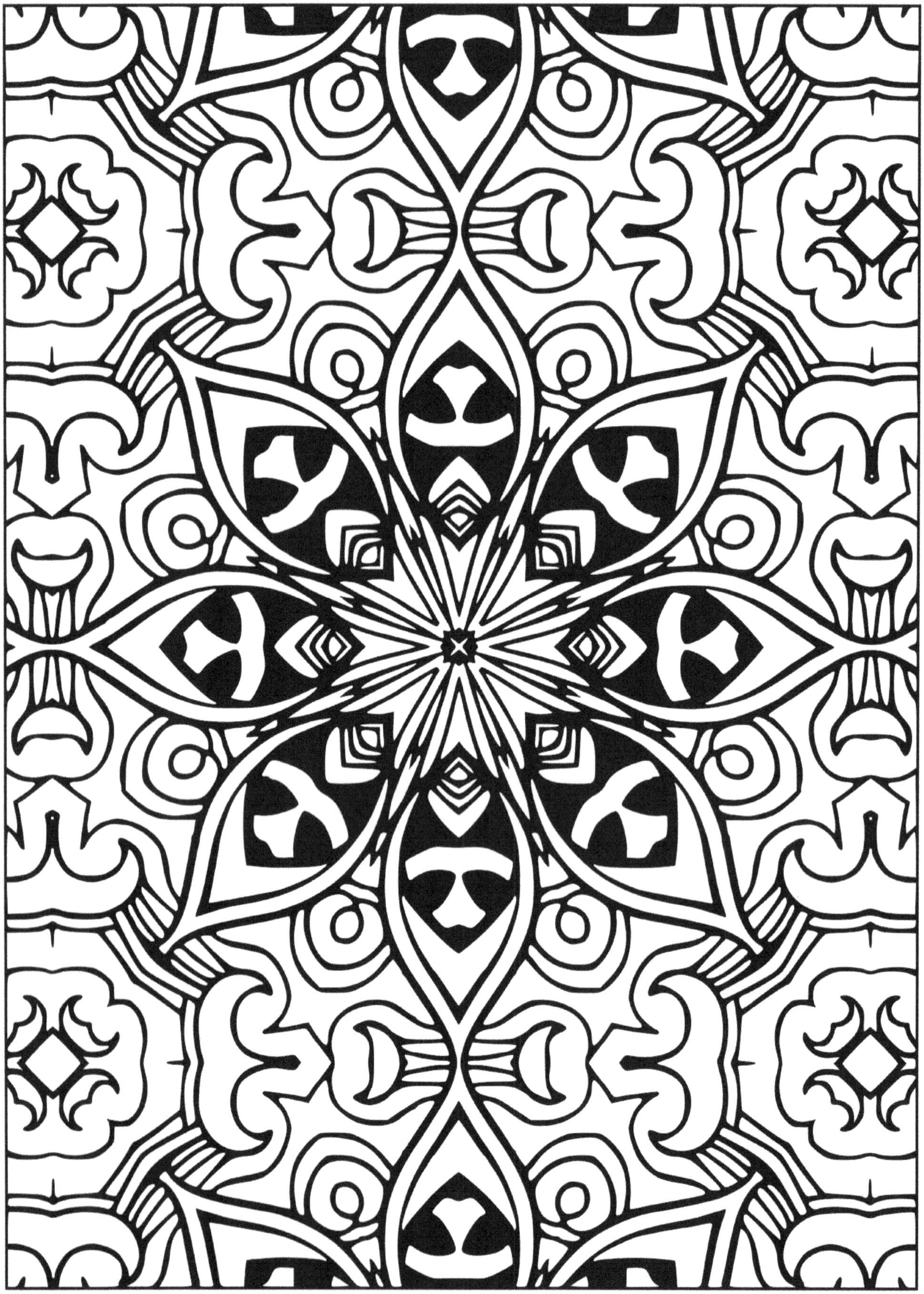

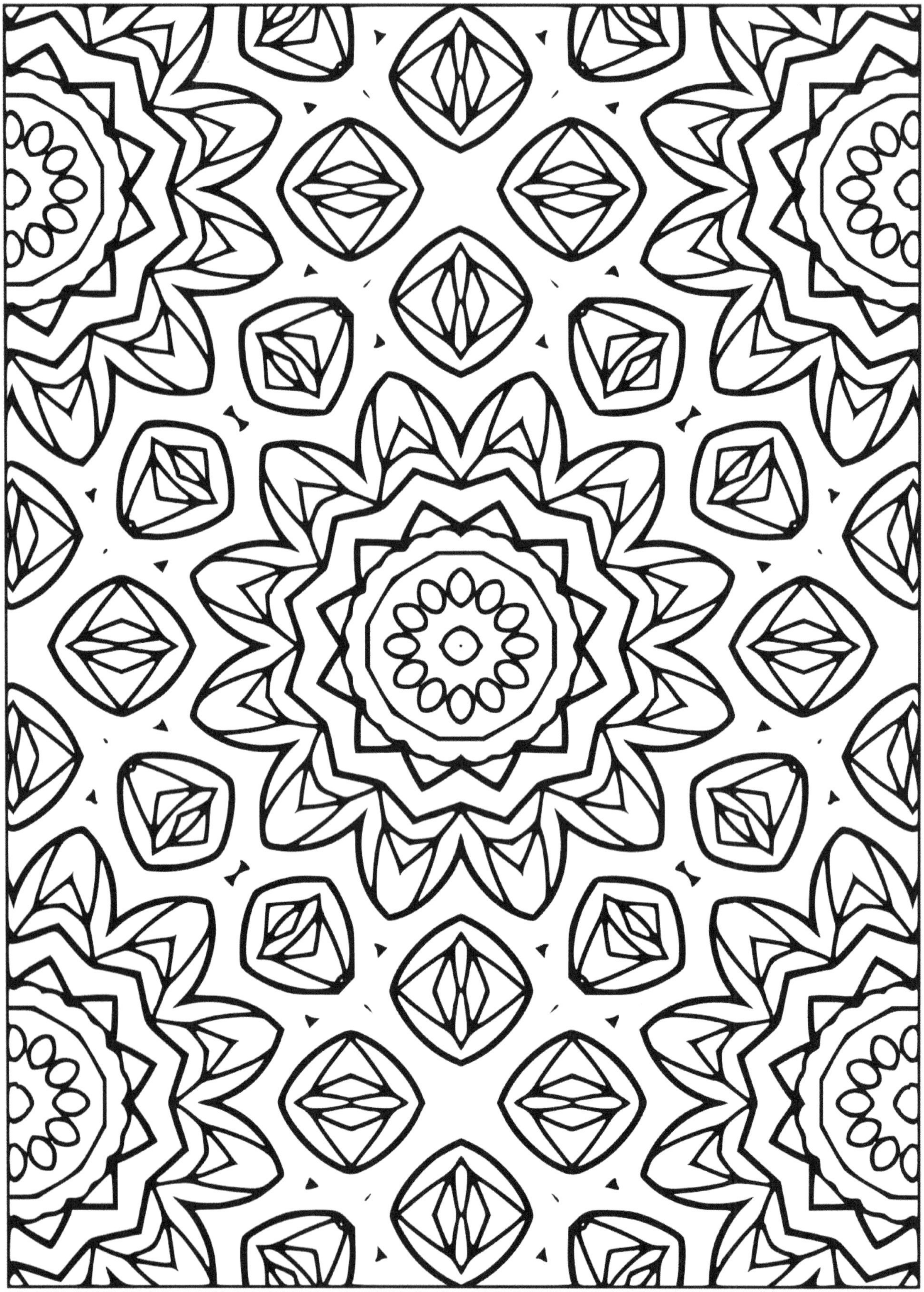

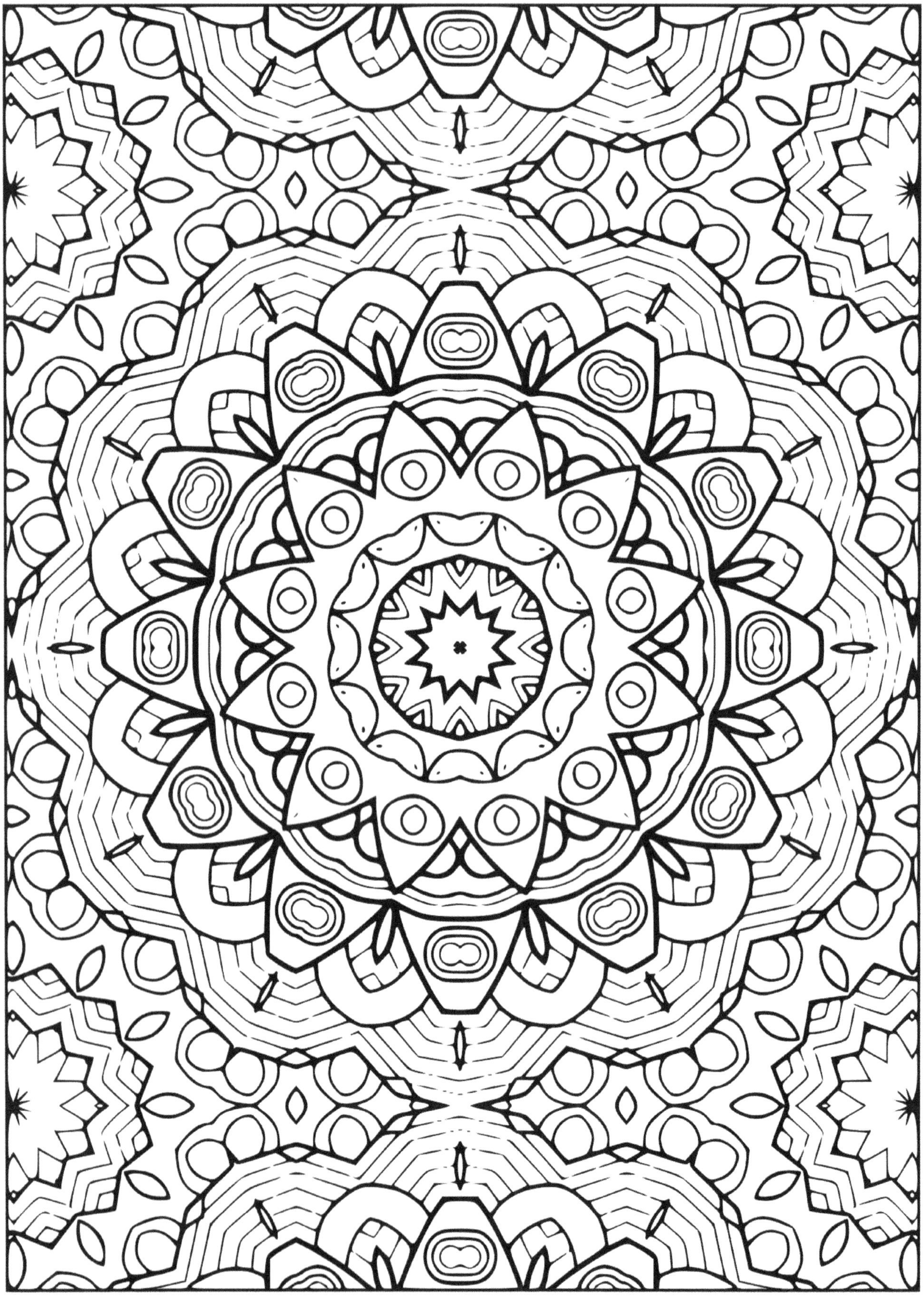

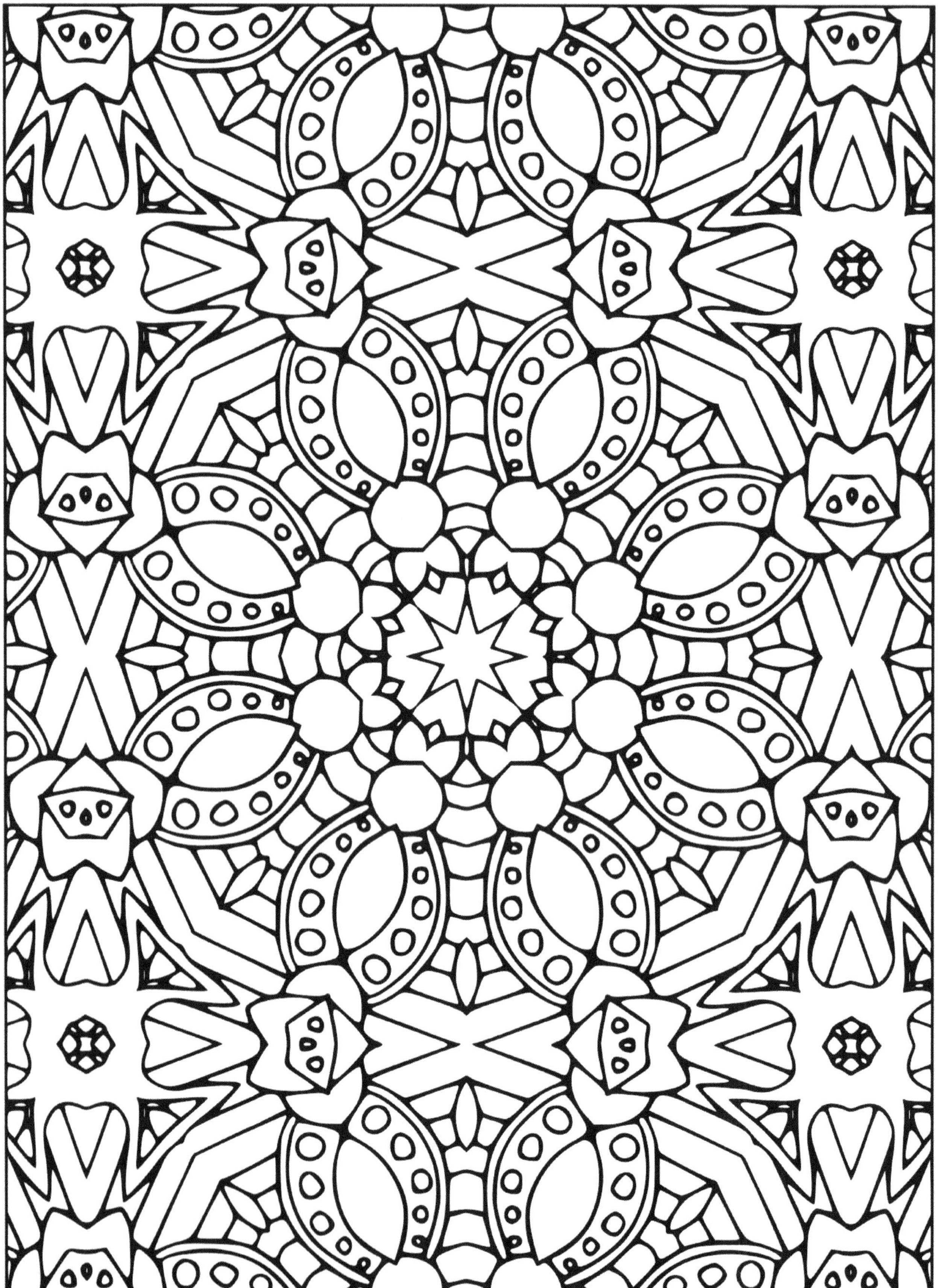

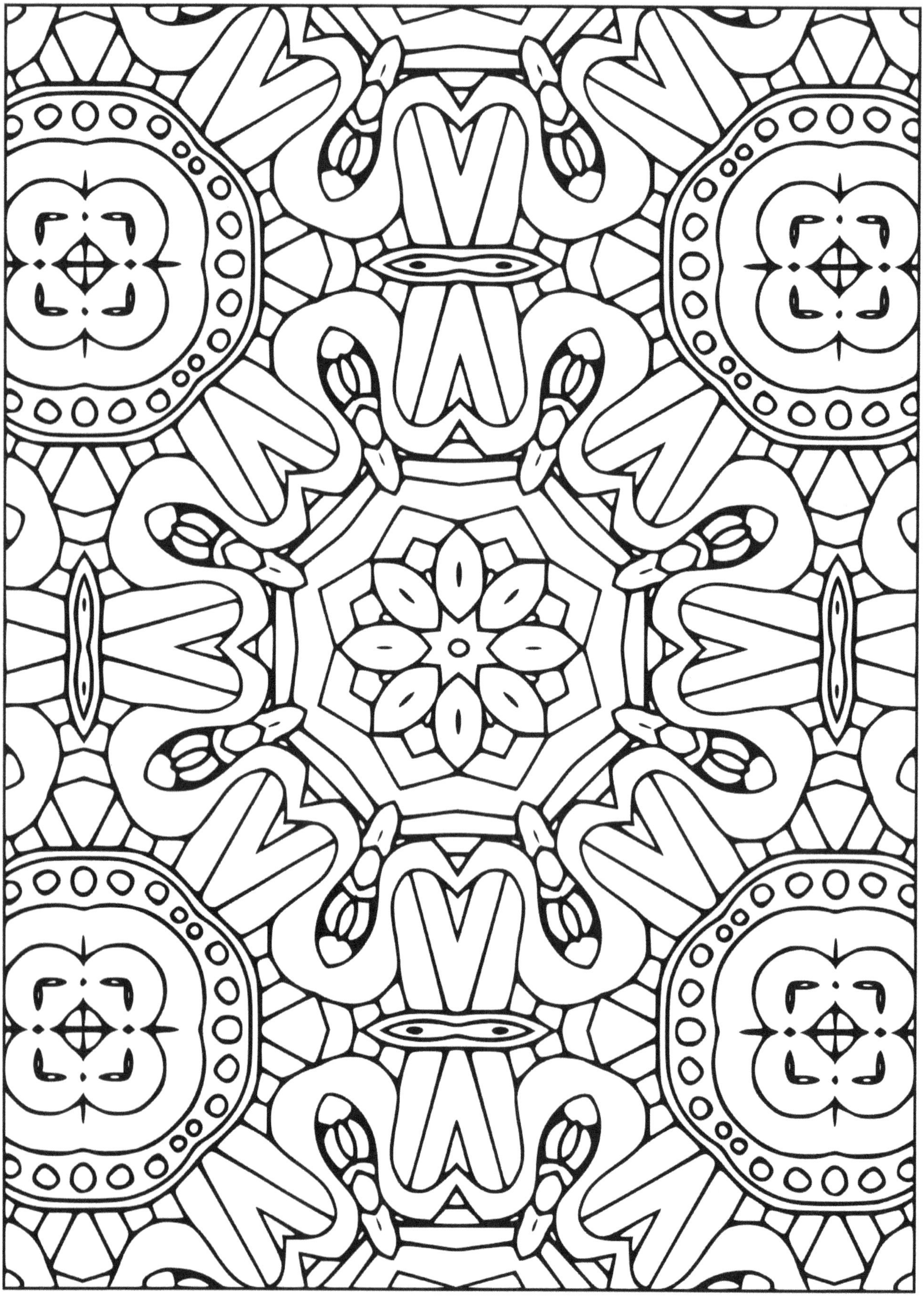

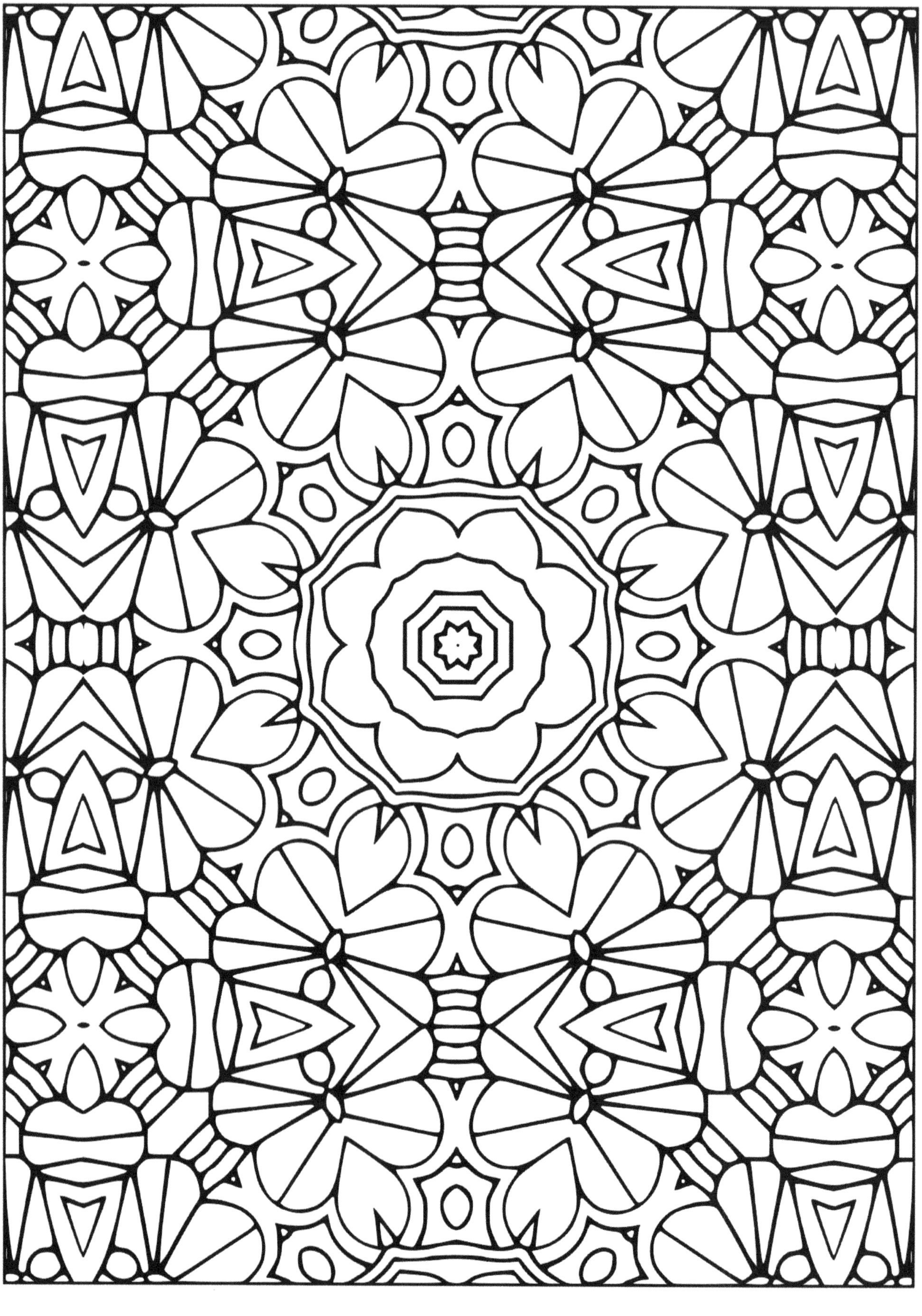

Lightning Source UK Ltd.
Milton Keynes UK
UKHW030628230720
367041UK00007B/504

9 781715 194628